CW01496763

Easy Almond Flour Recipes: Delicious Recipes for Breakfast, Lunch and Dinner

Scarlett Aphra

Legal Disclaimer

Contents

Easy Almond Flour Recipes:

Part One: Almond Flour Health Guide

About This Book

Welcome to Easy Almond Flour Recipes!

In this book you'll find a comprehensive beginner's health guide to almond flour and over a dozen easy recipes for learning to bake with almond flour. Part One of this book is designed to teach you all about almond flour: from its history to its practical applications in the kitchen. You'll learn how to bake with, store, and purchase almond flour, and the health benefits you can expect after incorporating it into your diet.

Part Two is designed to introduce you to baking with almond flour. The recipes range from breakfast to lunch and dinner, including family favorites like muffins, pancakes, and cookies.

Scarlett Aphra

At the end of this book, you should be comfortable purchasing and using almond flour in your daily diet!

What Is Almond Flour?

Almond flour is, quite simply, flour made from ground almonds. Although grainier than wheat flour, almond flour is still quite fine in texture. Almonds used for almond flour are usually blanched, which means the skin has been taken off.

There are three types of ground almond that are often used interchangeably when speaking about almond flour, but mean quite different things. These include almond flour, almond meal, and ground almonds. All are made from ground sweet almonds, but vary in texture and performance. Ground almonds will have a very coarse texture, almond meal will resemble corn meal, and almond flour – the one we're speaking about in this book – will have a very fine texture. The difference may seem small, but it is quite important for the recipes in Part Two.

Almond flour is used in baking, pastries, and candies, including French almond macarons, marzipan, and almond paste. Its use in baking is very common, especially with gluten free diets gaining popularity. Almond flour is great for quick breads, like muffins, banana bread, pancakes and waffles. It's very moist, with a great subtly nutty flavor, and is easy to use and purchase. You'll learn more about baking with almond flour a bit later in this section.

Who Can Use Almond Flour?

Almond flour has many uses, and is a perfect wheat flour substitute for many individuals. Almond flour is ideal for anyone looking to follow a diet low in carbohydrates, or looking to lower their cholesterol.

Being naturally gluten free, it's also ideal for individuals who have sensitivities or allergies to wheat and gluten. This includes those who have Celiac's disease and need to maintain a completely wheat and gluten-free diet.

Almond flour is also perfect for anyone who has chosen to adapt a vegan or vegetarian diet, as the flour is high in fats, proteins, and other vital nutrients and minerals.

Almond Flour Health Benefits and Nutritional Information

You've probably heard about the amazing health properties of almonds before, so it may not be much of a surprise just how healthy almond flour can be. Especially for those who can't tolerate gluten!

Almond flour harnesses the super health benefits of almonds, from protein content to minerals like magnesium. Almonds, although high in fat, are high in monounsaturated fats – these are the same fats are found in olive oil, and linked to a reduced risk of heart disease. They're also low in carbohydrates. It's believed that subbing nuts for an equivalent amount of carbs in an average diet will result in 30% reduction in the risk of heart disease. Almonds also lower cholesterol – specifically LDL cholesterol that is linked to heart disease.

Almonds have amazing antioxidant and blood stabilizing action, too. They contain vitamin E, and are high in magnesium and potassium. Almonds help stabilize rises in blood sugar after eating. A study published in the British Journal of Nutrition found that eating almonds reduced the glycemic index of a whole meal.

With all these incredible health benefits, it's no wonder people are beginning to include almond flour in their diets.

Almond Flour History

Almonds have a very long and rich history throughout the world, with recent popularity in North America thanks to California farms and an increased awareness in their health benefits.

Almonds originate from northern India, with their territory spanning over to Syria and Turkey. Their production spread from this region thousands of years ago along to the Mediterranean coast and into Africa and southern Europe. Almonds are recently grown in California, too – the only US state to grow the nuts, thanks to its incredible warm and temperate climate. In fact, 80% of the world's almonds are now grown in California!

Surprisingly, almonds are actually drupes, not a true tree nut. This means they are the seed of a fruit that grows on almond trees. Almond trees are mid-sized and bloom beautiful pink and white flowers. Mid-summer is the peak season for almond production, although they are available year-round.

Baking With Almond Flour

Almond flour is becoming a fast favorite among professional and home chefs, in part due to its nutritional benefits, its naturally gluten free nature, and its incredible taste.

Almond flour adds moisture and a rich taste to many recipes. It adds a nutty taste to baking, but not one that is overly obvious, allowing it to blend into many recipes well. It's a staple in French macarons, financiers, pie crusts, cookies, and more. It's also used in meatballs, or as breading/coating for chicken and fish.

In any recipe, you can replace one quarter of regular wheat flour with almond flour with no further changes, but beyond that the recipe will need to be adapted further. Because it contains no gluten, often times more eggs are needed in a recipe to act as a binding agent.

Almond flour should be kept in the freezer, but store some in the cupboard as well. Since the flour tends to clump straight out of the freezer, it's best to make sure you have some thawed on hand. Store this flour in a cool dry place in an airtight container.

Remember that recipes made with almond flour usually won't look like "normal" wheat flour batters – this is okay! Eventually, with enough practice, you'll learn what is considered normal for your almond flour baking. It's also best to let baked goods cool completely before eating.

Almond Flour vs. Other Flours

Although almond flour is gluten free, it is quite different from other gluten free flours and wheat flour. Almond flour has much more moisture and fat than wheat flour, and cannot be subbed in a 1:1 ratio. The recipes in this book are designed to work with almond flour specifically, sometimes alongside other gluten free flours.

Unlike some gluten free flours, like coconut flour, gluten free flour is very easy to find and sold in most grocery stores. Generally speaking, there is no need to go to a specialty shop or order online to find almond flour.

Easy Almond Flour Recipes:

Almond Flour Risks

The main risks for almond flour are spoilage and serious allergy. If you have, or suspect you have, an allergy to almonds, please do not consume almond flour without first consulting your physician.

Almond flour, due to its high fat content, tends to spoil relatively quickly. This is easily prevented by storing the flour in the freezer, with small batches kept in an airtight container for fast usage.

Buying and Making Almond Flour

Thanks to its increasing popularity, almond flour is easy to purchase both in stores and online. But it's important to know what you're looking for to ensure you buy the right flour for your needs. Although almond flour can be expensive, it is healthy and gluten free, and a great alternative to wheat flour, which makes it worth the higher price to many people.

When buying almond flour, check that unsweetened almonds are used, and that they are blanched. This ensures the best product with the finest texture for your baking. Check to make sure there are no other ingredients – you want to buy pure almond flour without other flours or additives involved. Check that the flour is gluten free, too, and the right texture. You don't want to start making a recipe to find that you've accidentally purchased almond meal by mistake. If unsure about the brand, read reviews or speak to staff about their opinion on the product.

Many people prefer to buy almond flour online to save money, as it can be on the pricy side in stores. When purchasing online, make sure you read reviews and trust the vendor or website. Remember to keep all your data secure!

You can also make it almond flour yourself, which can be an affordable and fun adventure. Detailed instructions for how to do this are in Part Two of this book.

Part Two: Almond Flour Recipe Guide

.

Things to Remember

Because almond flour does not react the same as wheat flour in recipes, there are a few things to keep in mind when baking with this gluten-free flour.

Sift and stir the flour thoroughly. Almond flour or meal can clump, especially when out of the freezer, so be sure to whisk, sift, or strain to get the best consistency.

Sub only 25%. When replace wheat flour in a recipe with almond flour, only substitute 25% of the flour. Since almond flour lacks gluten, the baking wouldn't stay together without additional binding agents, like eggs.

Follow the directions carefully. Baking with almond flour isn't always the same as baking with wheat flour. Be sure to read the directions fully before getting started.

Don't take directly from the freezer.
Always have some thawed, room temperature almond flour on hand. Almond flour straight out of the freezer will clump and perform poorly in recipes.

Scarlett Aphra

DIY Almond Flour
*makes almond milk, too

Ingredients
1 cup raw almonds, blanched
10 cups of water
1/2 tsp salt

Directions
In a large jug or bowl, soak the blanched almonds, along with the salt, in 3 cups of water for 12 or more hours.

Rinse the almonds, then toss them into a blender with at least 8 cups of water. Pulse on high until the almonds are grainy and everything is mixed smoothly. This will take 2-3 minutes.

Use a fine cheesecloth to strain the mixture into a jug or bowl, pouring the pulsed almond mixture through. The strained mixture is your almond milk; the pulp on top the cheesecloth will be your almond flour or meal.

Spread the pulp out evenly on a baking sheet lined with parchment, and bake in a very low oven (about 200F), for several hours, until the pulp dries. This will take several hours, but check the pulp frequently to avoid burning.

Allow it to cool, then pulse in a food processor again until the ideal fine texture. Be careful not to over pulse.

You now have a batch of almond four!

Beef Burgers

*(can be adapted into meatballs)

Ingredients
1 lb lean ground beef
2 eggs
1/2 onion, diced
2 garlic cloves, minced
1/2 cup almond flour
1/2 teaspoon salt
1/4 teaspoon pepper

Directions
Heat the barbecue to medium-high.
In a large bowl, combine the ground beef, eggs, flour, salt, and pepper. Using your hands, mix all the ingredients together until well combined.
Form patties, about the size of a hockey puck, and grill until cooked thoroughly, about 6 minutes each side.
The patties can be stored, uncooked, in the freezer between sheets of parchment.

Scarlett Aphra

Baked Lemon Donuts

Ingredients

Donut:

2 1/2 cups finely ground blanched almond flour plus more for preparing the pans

1/2 teaspoon baking soda

1/2 teaspoon salt

4 tablespoons honey

3 large eggs

1/4 cup canola oil

1 teaspoon pure vanilla extract

2 tablespoons lemon juice

2 tablespoon lemon zest, finely grated

Glaze:

2 cups icing sugar

3 tablespoons water

2 tablespoons lemon juice

Directions

Preheat oven to 350F and grease a standard donut pan.

In a medium bowl, combine the flour, baking soda, zest, and salt and mix.

In the bowl of a stand mixer, combine the honey, eggs, oil, vanilla, lemon juice, and mix until smooth.
 Gently stir in the flour mixture and beat until well combined.

Scoop the batter into the donut pan, about 2/3 full, and bake for 8-12 minutes, until golden brown. They should spring to the touch.

To make the glaze, whisk together the icing sugar, water, and lemon juice, adding more water if the mixture is too thick.

Easy Almond Flour Recipes:

While the donuts are still slightly warm, dunk them in the glaze and allow to drip on a wire rack.

Chocolate Chip Cookie Bars

Ingredients

2 1/2 cups almond flour

1/2 teaspoon salt

1 teaspoon baking soda

1/4 cup sugar

1/2 cup butter, melted

2 eggs

1 teaspoon vanilla

1 cup chocolate chips

Directions

Preheat oven to 350F, and grease a 9x13 baking pan.

In a medium bowl, combine the flour, salt, and baking soda.

In a large bowl, combine the butter and sugar, beating until creamy. Mix in the eggs and vanilla until smooth, then stir in the dry ingredients. Gently fold in the chocolate chips. Press the batter into the prepared baking pan, and bake for 18-20 minutes, until golden brown. Allow to cool completely before slicing.

Cinnamon Sugar Baked Donuts

Ingredients

Donut:

2 1/2 cups finely ground blanched almond flour

1/2 teaspoon baking soda

1/2 teaspoon salt

4 tablespoons honey

3 large eggs

1/4 cup canola oil

1 teaspoon pure vanilla extract

1 teaspoon cinnamon

1/4 teaspoon nutmeg

Coating:

1 cup sugar

1 tablespoon cinnamon

Directions

Preheat oven to 350F and grease a standard donut pan.

In a medium bowl, combine the flour, baking soda, and salt and mix.

In the bowl of a stand mixer, combine the honey, eggs, oil, and vanilla, and mix until smooth.

Gently stir in the flour mixture and beat until well combined.

Scoop the batter into the donut pan, about 2/3 full, and bake for 8-12 minutes, until golden brown. They should spring back to the touch.

To make the coating, stir together the cinnamon and sugar until well blended.

Allow the donuts to cool completely, then dunk them in the coating.

Scarlett Aphra

Chocolate Chip Cookie Bars

Ingredients

2 cups almond flour

1 teaspoon baking powder

1/2 teaspoon cinnamon

1/4 teaspoon sea salt

4 eggs

1/2 cup butter, melted

1/3 cup honey

1/4 cup low fat milk

1 teaspoon vanilla extract

1 cup blueberries, fresh or frozen

Directions

Preheat the oven to 350F, and grease or line a standard muffin tin.

In a large bowl, combine all the ingredients except for the berries. Stir until well blended, then gently fold in the berries.

Scoop the batter into the muffin tin, about 2/3 full each.

Bake for 18-20 minutes, until golden brown.

Basic Almond Flour Pastry

Ingredients

1 1/2 cups almond flour

1/2 cup icing sugar

3 tablespoons butter, frozen and cubed

3 tablespoons milk

Directions

Place the flour and icing sugar into a food processor, and pulse until smooth. Add the cubed butter and milk, and pulse until it becomes a workable dough.

Form the dough into two discs, cover in plastic wrap, and refrigerate for at least 20 minutes before using.

Scarlett Aphra

Almond Flour Oat Loaf

Ingredients

2 1/4 cup almond flour

1/4 cup flaxseed meal

2 teaspoon baking soda

1/2 teaspoon salt

3 eggs

2 tablespoon honey

2 tablespoons oats

Directions

Preheat oven to 300F and grease a standard loaf pan.

In a medium bowl, mix together the flour, flaxseed meal, salt, and baking soda.

In a large bowl, whisk together the eggs, and honey until smooth. Combine the wet and dry ingredients until well combined, and pour the batter into the pan.

Sprinkle with the oats and bake for 25-30 minutes.

Scarlett Aphra

Easy Chocolate Chip Cookies

Ingredients

3/4 cup almond flour

1/4 cup coconut flour

1 teaspoon baking soda

1/2 teaspoon salt

1/2 cup butter, melted and cooled

1/2 cup honey

1 teaspoon vanilla extract

1 cup chocolate chips

Directions

Preheat oven to 350F, and line a baking pan with parchment paper.

In a medium bowl, combine the flours, baking soda, and salt, and whisk until no lumps appear. Add the butter, honey, and vanilla, and mix until well combined. Fold in the chocolate chips.

Allow to sit for 10 minutes, then scoop 1.5 to 2 tablespoons of the dough onto the prepared pan. Bake for 10-12 minutes, until golden brown.

Scarlett Aphra

Blueberry Pancakes

Ingredients

1 1/2 cups almond flour

1 teaspoon baking powder

3 eggs

1 cup buttermilk

1 cup blueberries, fresh or frozen

Directions

In a medium bowl, whisk flour, eggs, and buttermilk until smooth.

Heat a skillet or griddle to medium, and when hot, pour 1/4 cup of batter for each pancake, place blueberries on top, and cook for 2 to 3 minutes each side, until golden brown.

Scarlett Aphra

Very Chocolate Cupcakes

Easy Almond Flour Recipes:

Ingredients
2 cups almond flour

1/3 cup unsweetened cocoa powder

1/2 teaspoon salt

1 teaspoon baking soda

1 cup honey

2 large eggs

1 tablespoon vanilla

Directions
Preheat oven to 350F, and grease or line a standard cupcake/muffin tin.

In a small bowl, stir together the flour, cocoa powder, salt, and baking soda, making sure there are no lumps.

In a large bowl, beat together the honey, eggs, and vanilla. Add the dry ingredients and mix until well combined.

Pour the batter into the prepared cupcake tin, filling each liner 2/3 full. Bake for 30-35 minutes, until a toothpick inserted in the center comes out clean.

Cinnamon Apple Rolls

Easy Almond Flour Recipes:

Ingredients
Pastry:

3 cups almond flour

1/2 teaspoon baking soda

1/2 teaspoon salt

1/4 butter, melted

2 eggs

1 tablespoon honey

Filling:

2 apples, finely chopped or grated

1/2 cup brown sugar

2 teaspoons cinnamon

2 tablespoons butter, melted

Directions
Preheat oven to 350F, and grease a muffin tin.

Mix the flour, baking soda, and salt in a medium bowl. Add the melted butter, eggs, and honey, and stir until well combined. Knead it a few times so it forms a firm dough.

Roll the dough into a large (about 14x14)

rectangle over a sheet of parchment. Combine the ingredients for the filling, and spread evenly over the dough, leaving 1 inch at the edges. Using the parchment as a helper, roll up the dough into a long log, like a jelly roll.

Slice the log into 1 to 2 inch pieces, and place in the muffin tins. Bake for 15 – 25 minutes, until golden brown.

Use your parchment paper to help roll it into a long log. You will need the assistance of your parchment paper, because this dough is made from almond flour it's not as stretchy and sticky as a wheat or other gluten flour.

Easy Almond Flour Recipes:

Oven Baked Chicken

Ingredients

3-4lbs chicken breasts, thighs, or drumsticks

3 eggs, beaten

1/2 cup Panko bread crumbs

1/2 cup almond flour or almond meal

1/2 teaspoon Italian herbs

1/2 teaspoon cayenne pepper

1/2 teaspoon salt

1/4 teaspoon pepper

Directions

Preheat oven to 425F and lightly grease a baking pan.

Place the beaten egg in one bowl, and the bread crumbs, herbs, and flour in another.

Dip the chicken pieces in the beaten egg, then in the flour mixture to coat evenly.

Bake until all pieces register 165F, about 30-40 minutes.

Scarlett Aphra

Double Chocolate Brownies

Easy Almond Flour Recipes:

Ingredients

3/4 cup almond flour

1/4 teaspoon salt

1/4 cup cocoa powder

1/2 teaspoon baking powder

1 cup sugar

1/2 cup butter

3 eggs

1 teaspoon vanilla

1 cup chocolate chips

Directions

Preheat oven to 350 degrees, and grease and flour an 8x8 baking pan.

In a medium bowl, combine the flour, salt, cocoa, and baking powder.

In a larger bowl, combine the eggs, sugar, vanilla, and butter. Beat in the dry ingredients until smooth. Fold in the chocolate chips.

Pour the batter into the prepared pan, and bake for 25-30 minutes, or until a toothpick comes out of the center with moist crumb

Scarlett Aphra

Mini Apple Pies

Ingredients

1 batch of pastry (see previous recipe)

2-3 apples, diced

1/3 cup brown sugar

1 tsp cinnamon

1/4 tsp nutmeg

1 Egg, beaten

Directions

In a medium bowl, mix together the apples, sugar and spices and allow to sit for at least 10 minutes.

Preheat the oven to 375F and line a baking sheet with parchment paper.

Roll out pie pastry until 1/4 inch or so thick. Use a large cookie cutter, or cutting around the rim of a bowl, cut out the pie shapes.

Place cut dough circles on the cookie sheet, and spoon 1 - 2 tbsp of filling in the middle, then fold in half. Press together the edges with fork, using water when needed to help it stick. Brush tops with the egg and bake for 25-35 minutes, until golden brown

Other Almond Flour Inspiration

By now you should have a clear idea of how almond flour can be used in a variety of recipes. Here are some more tips and tricks for adding almond flour to breakfast, dinner, and dessert.

> Replace 25% of the flour in any recipe with almond flour for an extra nutritional boost.

> Add almond flour or almond meal to smoothies, oatmeal, or pudding for a wonderful nutty flavor and nutritional addition.

> Try using almond flour in place of other gluten-free flours in your favorite recipes to see if the flavor becomes fuller and more robust.

ONE LAST THING

We would love to get your feedback about our book:

If you enjoyed this book or found it useful, we would be very grateful if you would post a short review on Amazon. Your support really does make a difference and we read all of the reviews personally, so we can get your feedback and make our books even better.

Thank you again for your support!

Sign up for free ebooks

Echo Bay Books is proud to bring you our latest and greatest eBooks on Amazon. We treat you as a guest, and we treat our guests well. We promise to only send you notifications if it has some goodies attached that we think you will like. We launch our eBooks for free for the first 5 days every time. That means you will be the first to know when new books launch (once per week) - for FREE. No spam, ever. Just follow this link http://eepurl.com/zYTDH and sign up!

5108824R00037

Printed in Great Britain
by Amazon.co.uk, Ltd.,
Marston Gate.